FESTIVALS

Meryl Doney

FRANKLIN WATTS
A Division of Grolier Publishing
LONDON • NEW YORK • HONG KONG • SYDNEY
DANBURY, CONNECTICUT

About this book

People all over the world celebrate festivals throughout each year. Some festivals are connected with religion and some with the local harvest, the planets, the weather, or important events in people's personal lives. The celebrations include family and public gatherings, eating and drinking together, making and displaying special decorations, wearing best clothes and jewelry, and generally having fun. Often weeks of preparation take place before the festivities begin, and in many countries whole industries have grown up to supply the items that festivalgoers need.

There are so many festivals held around the world that we cannot possibly mention them all. In this book, we have looked at some of the best-known or most spectacular ones.

They are drawn from different countries, cultures, and religions. On the left-hand pages you will see some of the wonderful items prepared for these festivals. On each right-hand page you will find detailed instructions for making one of the objects shown.

Most of the steps are very easy to follow, but where you see this sign ask for help from an adult.

All the preparations and the time spent making things are part of what makes any festival great. We hope you enjoy making the items in this book. You can make them on your own, or as part of a group, a school, or a club. And, most important, have fun celebrating!

© 1996 Franklin Watts
Text © Meryl Doney 1996

First American Edition 1997 by
Franklin Watts
A Division of Grolier Publishing Co., Inc.
Sherman Turnpike
Danbury, Connecticut 06813

10 9 8 7 6 5 4 3 2 1

Series editor: Kyla Barber
Editor: Jane Walker
Design: Visual Image
Cover design: Kirstie Billingham
Artwork: Ruth Levy
Photography: Peter Millard

Very special thanks to Myra McDonnell, advisor and model maker.

Library of Congress Cataloging-in-Publication Data

Doney, Meryl, 1942–
    Festivals/Meryl Doney.
    p.   cm. — (World crafts)
    Includes bibliographical references and index.
    Summary: Introduces a variety of well known festivals from around the world and provides instructions for related crafts, including a dragon toy for the Chinese New Year, dancing wings for Mardi Gras, and a sugar skull for Halloween.
    ISBN 0-531-14431-3 (lib.bdg)   ISBN 0-531-15329-0 (pbk)
    1. Handicraft—Juvenile literature.   2. Festivals—Juvenile literature.   [1. Festivals. 2. Handicraft.]   I. Title
II. Series: Doney, Meryl, 1942–   World crafts.
TT160.D67 1997
745.594'1—dc20   96-15838
                                                                    CIP AC

Printed in Great Britain

Contents

A year of festivals

People have celebrated festivals from the earliest times. Large fireplaces have been found inside caves where prehistoric people lived, suggesting that they used to gather together to eat and drink. We can also imagine them telling stories, making music to sing together, and getting up to dance.

Throughout history, people who live in the world's temperate regions have been affected by the different seasons. The seasons change as the Earth completes its path, or orbit, around the Sun during the year. All over the world, people celebrate these different seasons with festivals of light in the dark months and with dancing in the warmer, lighter times of the year.

The need to grow food plays a very important role in most societies. Sowing seeds, watering, and looking after crops take many long and back-breaking hours of work. Yet reaping the harvest and eating the food are times of joy and, hopefully, relaxation after all the hard work. Harvest festivals are special times of celebration.

Religion also has its important festivals. Some celebrate the birth of the founder of a religion. Others are events to remember in the stories of faith. Religious festivals can be a time to think about God or the gods, to put things right, to have sins forgiven, and to make a new start. Most of the greatest festivals held in the world are religious in origin. Each one has its own customs, foods, and special rituals. The activities that are part of these festivals are still important to many people throughout the world today.

A festivals resource kit

All the items in this book are very easy to make. If you plan to produce quite a few of them, you might like to collect together the most useful items of equipment and keep them in one place. Here are some recommended items for your festivals resource kit:

scissors • craft knife • pencil • brushes • tape measure • ruler • fabric paint • masking tape • poster colors • chalk • sewing pins •

safety pins • drawing pins • paper • newspaper • colored inks • felt-tip pens • stapler • iron and ironing board • needle and thread • sewing machine • tracing paper

Potato dough

This dough recipe is adapted from one in Peru. It is traditionally used for making retablo figures (see page 29), but it can be used instead of modeling clay to make all kinds of models.

You will need:
3 tablespoons of instant mashed potatoes
10 tablespoons of plaster of Paris
water

In a small bowl, mix up the mashed potatoes with 5 ounces (150 ml) of boiling water. Stir with a spoon until smooth.

In a larger bowl, mix the plaster with 3 tablespoons of cold water. Stir with a spoon until smooth and creamy.

Add the potatoes to the plaster and mix well. Form into a dough and knead.

No cooking is required for this dough, but it will dry quickly if left uncovered.

Salt dough

You will need:
2 cups of flour
$\frac{1}{2}$ cup of salt
$\frac{3}{4}$ cup of water

Mix the flour and salt together in a large bowl.

Make a well in the middle of the mixture, pour in a little water, and stir with a fork. Keep adding water, a little at a time, until you have used it all.

Finish mixing and kneading the dough with your hands. If it is too sticky, add more flour; if too dry, add more water.

Salt dough must be dried in the oven to become hard.

Happy New Year!

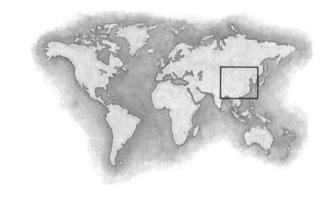

Chinese New Year is celebrated wherever in the world there is a Chinese community. New Year's Day occurs on the second new moon after the midpoint of the winter months, called the winter solstice. The festivities can last for many days. People clean their homes and often redecorate rooms in preparation. Food has to be cooked beforehand because some Chinese people believe that you should never use a knife on New Year's Day. You might cut your luck in two!

On New Year's Day, everyone is on their best behavior; they believe that any bad manners will continue throughout the year. Gifts are wrapped in red paper, with the words "new happiness for the New Year" written in gold.

The last day of the New Year celebrations is called the Lantern Festival. Lights like the one above, made from red paper, are hung everywhere. The highlight is the parade when a dragon, symbol of goodness and strength, weaves its way among the crowds. It is made from cane and paper, and may be so long that more than 50 people can dance underneath. Many children follow the dragon, carrying lanterns to light the way. They often hold small dragon toys like this one.

Make a Chinese dragon toy

You will need: three pieces of red construction paper, 13 x 4¹/₂ inches, 6¹/₂ x 6 inches, 8¹/₂ x 3 inches • pencil • tracing paper • scissors • black felt-tip pen • gold paint • strips of red and green construction paper, 1¹/₂ inch and ¹/₂ inch wide • sticky tape • glue • two corks • two garden sticks

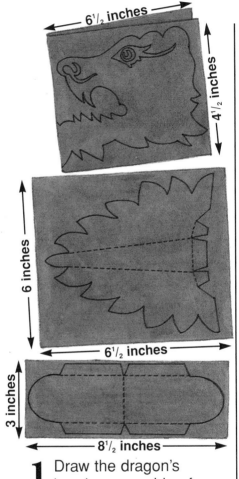

6¹/₂ inches

4¹/₂ inches

6 inches

6¹/₂ inches

3 inches

8¹/₂ inches

1 Draw the dragon's head on one side of the 13- x 4¹/₂-inch red construction paper. Trace the head a second time onto the other side. Draw the tail shape onto the 6¹/₂- x 6-inch paper. Draw the inside mouth on the 8¹/₂- x 3-inch paper.

2 Cut out and decorate head and tail with black felt-tip pen and gold paint.

3 To make body, cut one strip of 1¹/₂-inch red construction paper and one of 1¹/₂-inch green paper. Tape strips together at one end at right angles. Fold green strip over red strip, red over green, and so on to form an accordion. Join more red and green strips with tape, to form long body.

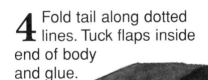

4 Fold tail along dotted lines. Tuck flaps inside end of body and glue.

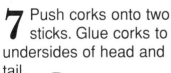

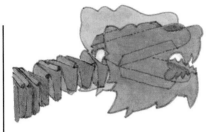

5 Fold inside mouth in half and fold flaps out. Tape to inside of head. Stick body to the head on the underside of mouth.

6 Make tongue from strips of ¹/₂-inch construction paper in same way as body. Cut ends to a point and glue inside mouth.

7 Push corks onto two sticks. Glue corks to undersides of head and tail.

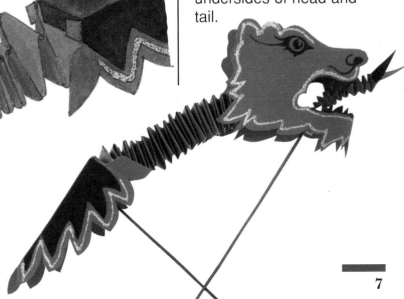

Mardi Gras

Carnivals are part of the traditional Christian year. They are held just before the period called Lent, when people stop eating certain foods in memory of Jesus Christ's fast for 40 days. The name "carnival" comes from the Latin words meaning "goodbye to meat." So just before this period of sadness and simple food, everyone dances and feasts.

In New Orleans in the United States, this celebration is called Mardi Gras, which is French for "Fat Tuesday." It is so named because people used up all their rich food before Lent. In some countries, the day is called Pancake Tuesday because people ate pancakes to use up their butter and eggs.

In the West Indies, especially in Trinidad, the famous steel bands lead the festival dancing with calypso music. They play on special "pans" made from used oil drums (right). In Rio de Janeiro, Brazil, dancers train all year for Mardi Gras. Each person wears a special outfit (see above). Some costumes are so elaborate that the wearers ride in the parade on a float!

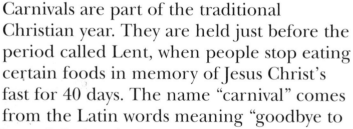

Make dancing wings

These wings are painted to look like a butterfly's. You could make your wings look like those of a bird, a moth, or a bat — or you could add any design you like.

You will need: tape measure • old sheeting or lining material • scissors • needle and thread • two ½-inch wooden dowels • newspaper • charcoal • large and small brushes • red, orange, yellow, and brown inks • gold paint • safety pin

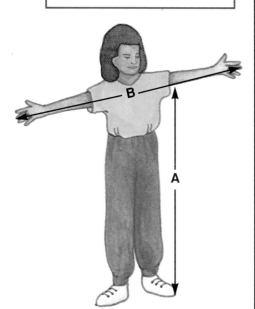

1 Measure yourself from under your arm to the floor (A). Measure from fingertip to fingertip across your back (B) and add 35 inches. Cut a piece of sheeting to these measurements.

2 Sew a narrow hem along the long side of the sheeting. Push a dowel into each end of this hem and secure with stitches.

3 Lay fabric on newspaper and draw pattern with charcoal. With a large brush and bold strokes, paint the butterfly onto the fabric with diluted inks. Begin with the red color, then let the orange blend in. Fill in the background with yellow. Make sure the ink soaks through to color both sides.

4 With a smaller brush, paint details in brown ink. When dry, add the "eyes" with gold paint. Cut around edges of wings.

5 To wear wings, pin middle of sheeting to the back of your collar. Hold a dowel in each hand and lift wings up and down.

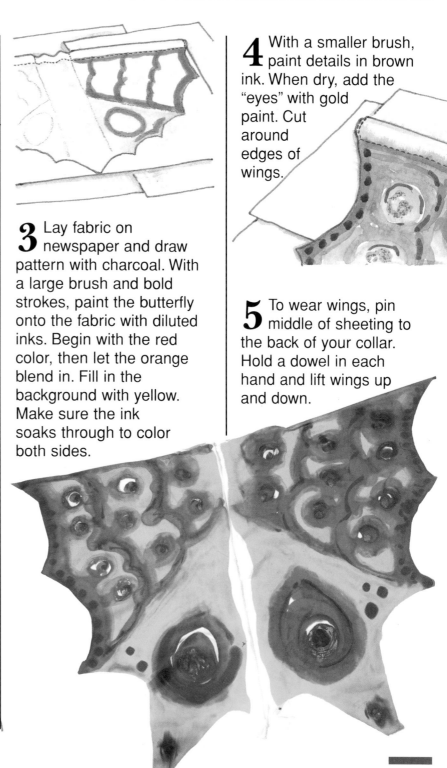

PAKISTAN

The *Eid* festivals

Muslims celebrate two festivals which date from the time of their prophet Muhammad, who lived about 1400 years ago. These two festivals are *Eid-ul-Fitr* and *Eid-ul-Adha*. They are kept by Muslims all over the world.

Eid-ul-Fitr means "the day which returns often." It is held on the day of the new moon at the end of Ramadan. The month-long period of Ramadan involves a fast that every devout Muslim undertakes once a year. During Ramadan no food is eaten between daybreak and sunset. This period ends in a joyful festival, when Muslims wear their best clothes and visit friends and relatives. Gifts and cards like the ones below from Pakistan are exchanged. The greeting is *Eid Mubarak*, which means "blessed *Eid*."

The other major Islamic festival is *Eid-ul-Adha*, which is held during the pilgrimage to the Muslim holy city of Mecca, as well as in other parts of the world where Muslims live. It recalls the story of the prophet Ibrahim, who was willing to sacrifice his son Isaac to Allah (God). Allah provided a ram in the boy's place, and Ibrahim's beloved son was spared.

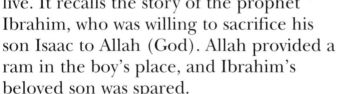

Make your own *Eid* card

You could use this method to make your own holiday card design. You could make an envelope from the same colored paper, too.

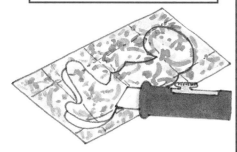

1 Fold the construction paper in half. Trace the dotted outline of the writing above onto the wrapping paper as shown. Cut along outline with a craft knife.

2 Glue wrapping paper to front of construction paper. Trace the Arabic writing onto the construction paper in the middle of the cut shape. Cut out the writing with a craft knife (or paint the words in gold paint).

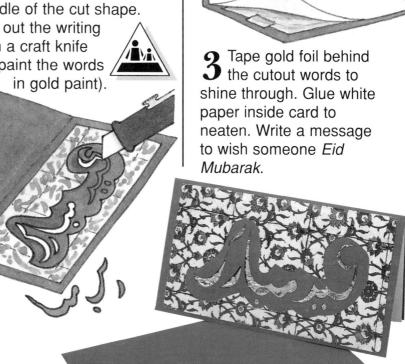

3 Tape gold foil behind the cutout words to shine through. Glue white paper inside card to neaten. Write a message to wish someone *Eid Mubarak*.

Easter

The word "Easter" comes from the pre-Christian celebration in honor of Eostre, the goddess of spring. Today, this festival is best known as a Christian celebration of the resurrection of Jesus Christ. It celebrates rebirth and new life. Eggs, which are traditionally a symbol of life, have become an important part of Easter celebrations.

In France on Easter morning, people ring bells to tell the children to start searching for eggs hidden in the house or garden. In Germany, the Easter hare, another symbol of spring, hides children's eggs in birds' nests. Papier-mâché eggs, like these from Germany (below: far right and top center), are filled with sweets or gifts and hidden for the children to find.

The art of decorating eggs goes back hundreds of years. The egg is either hard-boiled or the insides are blown out. It is then dyed and colored like these (below: bottom row) from the Ukraine. Some of the most gorgeously decorated eggs were made for the Russian czar by the famous jeweler, Fabergé. Every year he made a beautiful egg casket, such as the one shown top left, to hold the czar's Easter gift to his wife. Today, his designs are copied for gift eggs like the tin one (far left).

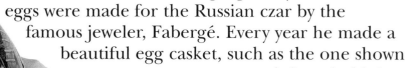

Make a Fabergé-style egg

You could fill this papier-mâché egg with chocolates or Easter eggs to make a perfect Easter gift.

You will need: modeling clay • knife • wooden board • water • paper • white glue • brush • scissors • stretchy fabric • fabric glue • ribbon • plastic jewels or sequins • thick needle • thin gold cord

1 Form a large egg out of modeling clay. Cut it in half and lay both halves, cut side down, on a board.

2 Wet the clay with water and cover with a layer of small pieces of wet paper. Paint white glue over this layer and add another layer. Continue adding layers and glue until you have built up a thick shell. Let dry.

3 Ease shells off their molds. Trim the edges carefully.

4 Stretch fabric over each shell and glue around the inside rim. Glue ribbon around the outside edge and fold inward. Glue to neaten.

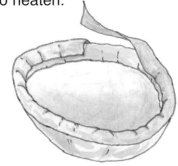

5 Decorate by gluing gold cord and plastic jewels or sequins to the egg's surface.

6 Use a needle to pierce four holes in each egg half, two on each side. Thread one piece of cord through one set of holes on each half to act as a hinge. Cord can be threaded through the holes on the other side and tied.

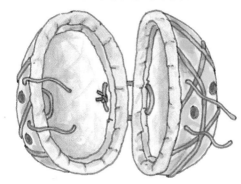

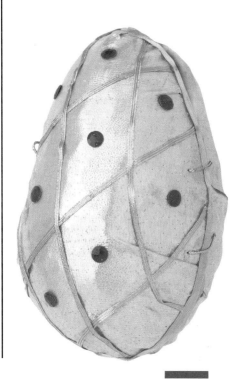

Welcome spring!

Every country has its own traditional celebrations for the beginning of spring. In India, the Hindu festival of *Holi* begins with a bonfire to celebrate the death of Holika, the demon of winter. On the next day, the fun begins. People throw handfuls of colored powder or spray each other with colored water. The festivities continue with feasting and dancing, when these decorated sticks (below) are used. Then comes *Chaitra*, the first month of spring, when people welcome the New Year with banners and gifts of sweets.

In Christian countries, spring is largely associated with Easter, but many pagan (not religious) festivals also remain. In country villages, young girls still dance around the maypole, a tall pole decorated with flowers and ribbons. The dance is meant to encourage the harvest of the newly sown crops. The "green man" (above) is an ancient symbol of the strong links between people and the earth. Some old churches still have carvings of the pagan green man at the top of pillars, and pubs named "The Green Man" are a reminder of this rural past.

Make a green-man mask

The process of scoring construction paper makes it possible to fold it easily, especially along curved shapes. Draw the shape you need on the construction paper in pencil. Then draw the blade of a craft knife gently along the line, cutting the surface but taking care not to pierce right through it.

You will need: plain construction paper, 11 x 14 1/2 inches • pencil • scissors • craft knife • hole punch • thin green ribbon • two sheets of construction paper (different greens) • sticky tape

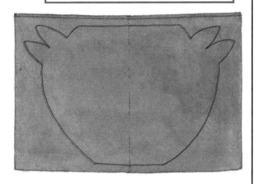

1 Fold plain construction paper in half. Draw mask shape as shown, and cut out.

Hold mask against your face, and mark the position of your eyes and mouth with a pencil.

2 With a craft knife, cut eyes and mouth. Make slits between eyes and down nose. Punch two sets of holes on each side. Thread ribbon through holes.

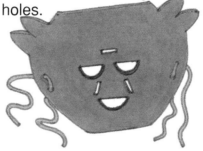

3 Cut out eight leaves from the green paper. Score down the lines. Fold leaves, accordion style, so each one stands out.

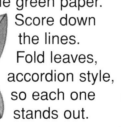

4 Cover the mask with leaves. Push the stems through the slits and into the mouth. Tape stems firmly in place on the back.

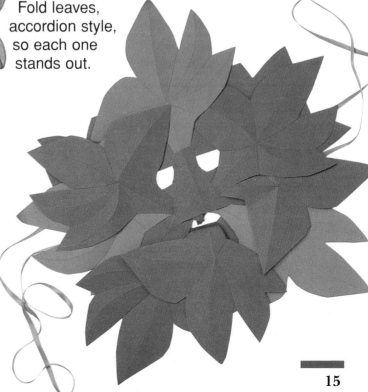

Honoring the ancestors

In many cultures, it is very important to show respect for your ancestors and to honor them regularly. People call on their brave heroes and heroines of the past to help them during times of need. When Europeans began their conquest of North America, the Native Americans used to perform a ghost dance to call upon past warriors to help them. They wore special shirts like the one shown (right). Sometimes the shirts had handprints on them to ward off the white man's bullets.

Chinese people greatly respect their ancestors and send useful articles to their dead relatives. These items are sometimes quite complicated models made out of paper. The models are then burned as a way of sending them to the life beyond. A special festival is held at the beginning of winter when cold-weather clothes made from paper, or the money to buy them (shown below), are burned. Unfortunately, the money is of no use on earth as it can only be used in the afterlife.

Make afterlife banknotes

To make your banknotes look like an impressive wad, cut sheets of newspaper to the same size and stack them into a pile. Put one printed note on top and one on the bottom. Secure with a rubber band.

You will need: wooden photo frame • silk or nylon fabric (to fit over frame) • stapler • paper • red and green pencils • two pieces of thin paper • craft knife • newspaper • white paper to print on • pencil • tubes of red and green gouache paint • rubber gloves • short ruler • felt-tip pen

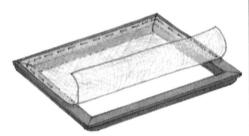

1 To make screen, stretch fabric over back of frame. Staple in place.

2 Draw a simple banknote design in red and green pencil. Trace red areas onto one sheet of thin paper, and green areas onto the other sheet. With a craft knife, cut out traced areas to make two stencils.

3 Spread out newspaper and place white paper on top. Lay red stencil on paper. Mark edge of stencil with a pencil.

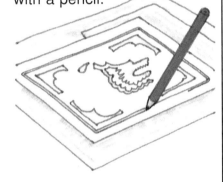

4 Cover stencil with screen. Mark edge of screen with pencil.

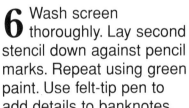

5 Squeeze red paint onto screen and draw it over surface with ruler. Raise screen. Stencil should stick to it. Remove first printed note and let it dry. Repeat as often as stencil will allow. Remove screen and stencil.

6 Wash screen thoroughly. Lay second stencil down against pencil marks. Repeat using green paint. Use felt-tip pen to add details to banknotes.

Everyday celebrations

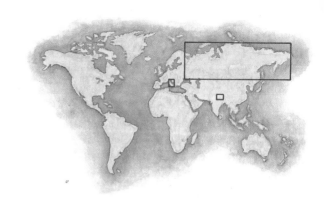

People can celebrate their faith on a daily basis by carrying special objects around with them, or by keeping them around the home. In orthodox Christian homes, for example in Russia, a corner of the house is reserved for a shrine with holy pictures, called icons (below left), on the wall.

Prayer is a universal way in which people communicate with their God or gods. Catholic Christians use a rosary like the one shown below right from Italy, to help them pray through a series of prayers, one bead at a time. Prayer beads are sometimes used by Muslims, Buddhists, and Hindus. The set in the center is called a *chursa*, and comes from Tibet.

In Tibet, regular praying is so important that prayers are often rolled into tall cylinders and placed outside temples. The worshiper turns the cylinders instead of speaking the prayers. Prayers are also written on long, thin flags so the wind will read them constantly. The cylinder (right) is a hand-turned version called a prayer wheel. The worshiper swings the cylinder containing the prayers around in a circle.

Make a prayer wheel

You will need: cardboard mailing tube, 3 inches wide, with metal or plastic end • thick cardboard • scissors • glue • 39-inch bamboo stick • two corks • smaller cardboard tube, 8½ x 1 inches • self-hardening modeling clay • thin gold cord • decorative button • gold paint • gold braid • glue • plastic jewels • varnish • paper • pencil

1 To make drum, cut 3 inches from the end of the cardboard tube. Make a lid by cutting out a disk just a little bigger than the tube. Cut another disk slightly smaller than the inside of the tube. Glue disks together.

2 Make handle by pushing stick into a cork. Push cork into small cardboard tube.

3 Mold a weight from clay. Make a hole in the weight. Pierce two holes in the side of the drum. Thread cord through the drum holes and the weight. Tie on the inside of the drum.

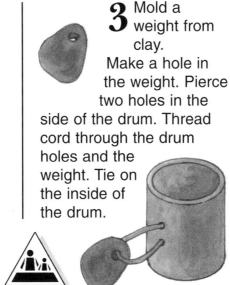

4 To assemble drum, pierce a hole in the base and lid. Fit lid onto drum. Push stick through both holes in drum. (Make sure the drum turns freely.)

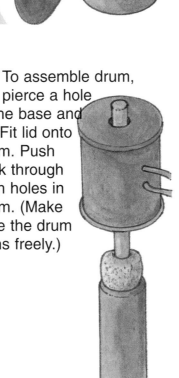

5 Push second cork onto end of stick and glue button on top. Paint gold. Glue on gold braid and plastic jewels. Varnish.

6 If you want to, write a prayer on a long, thin piece of paper. Roll it up and place inside drum. Swing the weight around to turn the prayer wheel.

ISRAEL, UNITED STATES, AND BRITAIN

Harvest festivals

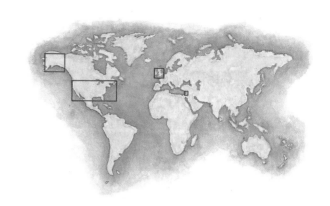

People who live in cities may have lost contact with the yearly harvest of food crops, yet festivals are still held to remind us just how important these events are. In Israel there are spring, summer, and autumn harvests. The harvest festival in September is called *Sukkot.* This special market in Jerusalem (right) has been set up for the festival of *Sukkot.*

Thanksgiving Day in the United States dates back to the time when the first settlers from England celebrated their survival during the first year in their new country. Families and friends get together for a meal of turkey, pumpkins, corn, cranberries, and sweet potatoes — the foods that the Native Americans introduced to the settlers.

In Britain, harvest festivals are mostly celebrated in Christian churches. An old tradition is to bake a loaf in the shape of a wheat sheaf (left), using the last of the harvested grain. The loaf is taken to the decorated church as a symbol of thanksgiving for the harvest.

Make harvest loaf paperweights

These little loaves make good gifts. Mark the person's name in the band across the middle before you bake them. If you prefer to make loaves that you can eat, use bread dough instead of salt dough and follow a recipe for making bread.

You will need: 1 cup plain flour • 1 cup salt • bowl • water • fork • wooden board • blunt knife • oven • varnish • brush

1 Mix the flour and salt in a bowl. Add water slowly, mixing with a fork, until a firm dough is formed.

2 Pull off a hand-sized lump and roll into a ball on the board. Press with your hand to form an oblong shape.

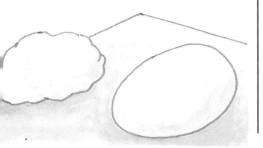

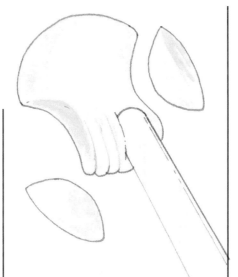

3 With a blunt knife, cut away the sides of the dough to form a wheat sheaf shape. Cut stalk lines in the bottom half.

4 With more dough, make a long, thin roll. Break off small pieces and roll ends to points. Press these into top half, in diagonal rows, to form wheat grains. Lay a flat piece of dough around waist of sheaf.

5 Let the dough rise a little. Cook in medium-hot oven until as hard as a cracker. Varnish when cold.

Halloween and All Souls' Day

The period from October 31 to November 2 is celebrated by Christian communities as the time when people remember those who have died. All Hallows' Eve, or Halloween ("hallows" means holy), has become associated with ghosts and spirits who come back to haunt the living.

In Mexico, there is a widespread folk tradition of ancestor worship, but the Catholic religion is also very strong. All Souls' Day is celebrated as the Day of the Dead, when people visit the graves of their relatives, often singing, dancing, and feasting there. Days are spent preparing for this fiesta. Sugar model-making dates back over 100 years and has developed into a remarkable skill. Elaborate skeletons and skulls (see above), coffins, saints, and animals are made from sugar for the children to enjoy. They are formed in hollow shapes out of hard white sugar and decorated with bright colors.

In North America and parts of Europe, a traditional symbol of this season is the pumpkin head. The pumpkin is hollowed out, carved with a scary face, and then used as a lantern. (All the visiting spirits must leave the earth again by All Saints' Day on November 1.) The North American tradition of trick or treat comes from the original idea that you must be kind to dead ancestors or they will play tricks on you.

Make a sugar skull

You will need: ready-to-roll white icing or fondant icing • wooden board • round-bladed knife or modeling tool • cake decorations • food coloring • brush

This skull is not hollowed out in the same way as a Mexican sugar skull, but made from prepared icing, which is easier to use. It will be too sweet to eat all at once, so make your skulls small or share them with lots of people!

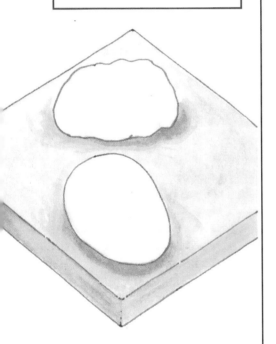

1 Knead the icing until it is soft enough to model. Pull off a small piece and roll it into a ball. Press down onto a board to form a flat-bottomed egg shape.

2 At the narrower end, squash in the sides to form cheek bones.

3 Use both ends of the knife or modeling tool to form the features. Halfway down, press in the eye sockets. Below these, form two nostril holes. Make teeth shapes along the bottom of the jaw.

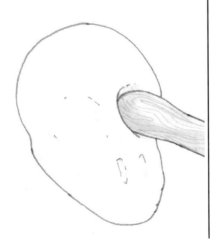

4 Let the icing sugar harden. Paint the features with food coloring. Decorate with cake decorations.

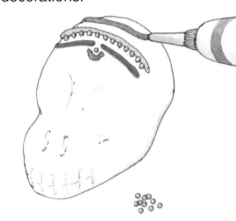

Founder's Day

Most religions hold very special festivals in honor of their founders. *Wesak* is the Mahayana Buddhists' celebration of the life of Buddha (Mahayanan, or western, Buddhism is strongest in Burma, Thailand, Kampuchea, and Laos). *Wesak* falls on the full moon in April or May. The Buddha's birth, his first steps, his enlightenment under a bodhi tree, and his entry into *nirvana* are all commemorated. Cards like the ones shown below are exchanged during the festival.

In India, Sikhs celebrate the birth of their founder, the guru Nanak, and of nine other important gurus. The main part of these celebrations is the Akhand Path, which is a continuous three-day reading of the Adi Granth, the Sikh scriptures. Special garlands are worn or draped over the portraits of the gurus as a sign of respect. The design in the center of the one below is the Sikh symbol, *ek onkar.*

Make a portrait garland

This garland has a picture of guru Nanak in the center, but you could use the same method to make a garland celebrating any festival that is important to you.

You will need: thin cardboard, 7 x 8 inches • pencil • scissors • picture of guru • glue • needle and thread • 5 feet gold tinsel • pins • 10 feet red ribbon, $1\frac{1}{4}$ inches wide • 3 feet gold gift-wrap ribbon • 14 inches thin ribbon

1 Draw a shield shape on the cardboard. Glue picture of the guru in the middle. Cut out shield.

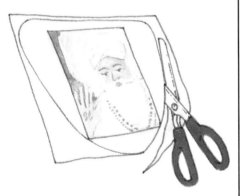

2 Cut off 5 feet of red ribbon. Sew a running stitch along the center. Pull thread to gather ribbon so that it fits around shield.

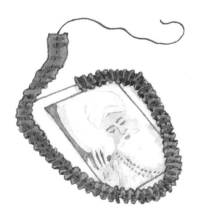

3 Cut enough tinsel to edge shield and lay on the cardboard. Pin in place. Lay gathered ribbon on top and pin through tinsel. Sew through all layers to hold in place. Remove pins.

4 Cut two $17\frac{1}{2}$-inch lengths of tinsel, red ribbon, and gift-wrap ribbon. Sew ribbons together to make two straps. Sew tinsel down middle.

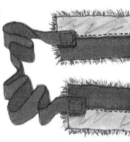

5 Sew straps to top of shield. Sew thin ribbon to ends of straps to complete the garland.

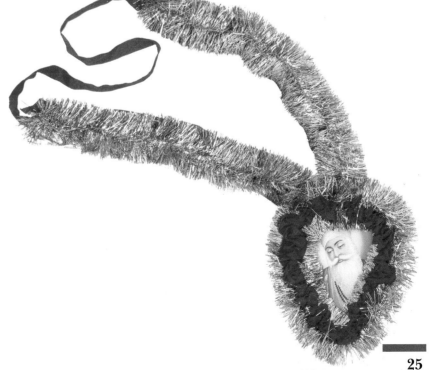

Festivals of Light

In India, Diwali is the major Hindu festival of light. The name comes from *deepawali*, which means "a row of lights." It is celebrated around the months of October and November and marks the beginning of the New Year for many people in India. The festival lasts for several days, with fireworks and parties. Little clay lamps are made (below left), and set in rows in windows to mark the return from banishment of Rama and Sita, the hero and heroine of the Indian sacred text, *Ramayana*.

The Jewish festival of light falls in December and is called Hanukkah. It commemorates the relighting of the *menorah*, the seven-branched candlestick in the temple at Jerusalem in 168 B.C. At that time the oil for the temple lamps miraculously burned for eight days. The festival lasts for the same length of time. During the festival, one of the eight candles on the candlestick (right), is lit every day. The ninth candle is used to light the others. Parties are held, special food is served, and the children play a game with a spinning top called a dreidel (below center). It has four sides, each with a Hebrew letter standing for the words "a great miracle happened here."

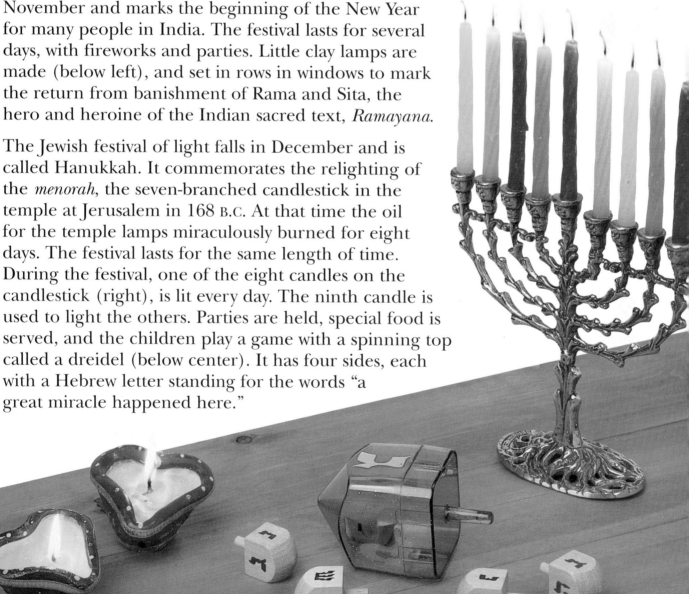

Make Diwali lights

1 Pull off a piece of clay the size of a golf ball. Roll it into a ball. Push your thumb into the center. Pinch and turn the clay to make a small thumb pot.

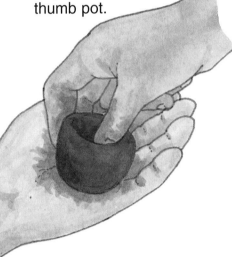

2 Press the walls of the pot thinner until you can fit a night light in the bottom.

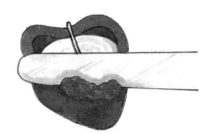

3 Mold the pot into a heart shape around the night light. Trim the top of the rim flat.

4 Roll out a thin sausage of clay and lay it around the edge of the pot. Let it dry hard.

5 Paint the inside and outside of the pot in bright colors. Decorate it with dots and dashes.

6 Varnish it for a shiny finish. Glue cord around the top and base and glue sequins around the middle.

Christmas

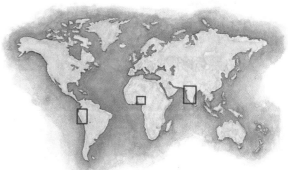

In Roman times, the winter solstice was celebrated with the Saturnalia, a feast in honor of the god Saturn. When Christianity was adopted by the Romans, the Christ Mass (Christmas), which commemorated the birth of Jesus, took over from this popular festival.

Many traditions surround the celebration of Christmas. Families get together, eat a special meal, and give each other presents. Christians go to church for special services, and there is often a crib or nativity scene in the church. The carved wooden nativity scene (bottom right) comes from a Christian church in southern India, and the stable scene behind it is from Nigeria.

In Peru, *retablos* with nativity scenes inside are very popular. When Christianity was first taken to South America, traveling priests carried small altars around with them for festival days. These gradually developed into portable boxes with saints above the altar and scenes from everyday life below it. Today, Christmas *retablos* like the ones shown here (below left) depict Mary, Joseph, and baby Jesus, with local people crowding around.

Make a *retablo* scene

This *retablo* will make a lovely centerpiece for Christmas, but you may prefer to make one showing scenes from your own surroundings. You could add characters representing your family or friends in the bottom section.

You will need: large sheet corrugated cardboard • pencil • craft knife • masking tape • two thin oblong boxes (such as toothpaste) • strong glue • two strips cotton fabric • soft white paper • white glue • water • poster paints • brush • modeling clay or potato dough (see page 5) • flat board • varnish

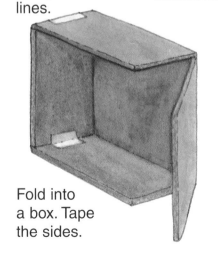

1 Draw the box pattern on the corrugated cardboard. Use a craft knife to cut around the edges and score along the dotted lines.

Fold into a box. Tape the sides.

2 Cut out two pieces for doors and a triangle for the front. Cut oblong boxes and fit them inside as "steps."

3 Glue triangle to roof. Glue cotton fabric strip down side of each door to form hinge. Attach to sides of box.

4 Cover whole box with a layer of papier-mâché (see page 13). Paint the outside white and the inside dark blue and green. Decorate the outside.

5 Use clay or potato dough to make the model figures. Work on a flat board. Let dry. Paint with poster paints. Varnish for a glossy finish.

6 Glue figures in position. Group shepherds and kings together. Make sure they face opposite ways. Baby Jesus should face forward.

Useful information

Museums

American Craft Museum
40 West 53rd Street
New York, NY 10019
Tel: 212-956-3535
Fax: 212-956-3699
(American 20th-century crafts by artists working in glass; textiles; wood; ceramic and metal media)

Cooper-Hewitt National
Museum of Design
Smithsonian Institution
2 East 91st Street
New York, NY 10128
Tel: 212-860-6868
Fax: 212-860-6909
(design and decorative arts of all periods and countries; architecture and design drawings; textiles; wallpaper; prints; graphics; woodwork; metalwork; ceramics; glass; furniture)

Museum of American Folk Art
61 West 62nd Street
New York, NY 10023
Tel: 212-977-7170
Fax: 212-977-8134
(American 18th- to 20th-century folk sculpture and painting; textile arts; decorative arts; environmental folk art; history)

Organizations

American Craft Council
72 Spring Street
New York, NY 10012
Tel: 212-274-0630
Fax: 212-274-0650

National Council on Education
for the Ceramic Arts
P.O. Box 1677
Bandon, OR 97411
Tel: 503-347-4394

North American Committee of
Enamel Creators
P.O. Box 96
Rockport, MA 01966
Tel: 508-546-6930

Books

Christmas Crafts
by Judith Hoffman Corwin
(Watts, 1996)

Christmas Fun: Holiday Crafts and Treats
by Diane Cherkerzian
(Boyds Mills, 1994)

Every Day is Earth Day
by Kathy Ross
(Millbrook, 1995)

Crafts for Halloween
by Kathy Ross
(Millbrook, 1994)

Crafts for Kwanzaa
by Kathy Ross
(Millbrook, 1994)

Crafts for Valentine's Day
by Kathy Ross
(Millbrook, 1995)

Easter Crafts
by Judith Hoffman Corwin
(Watts, 1994)

Halloween Crafts
by Judith Hoffman Corwin
(Watts, 1995)

Handmade Christmas Gifts That Are Actually Usable
by Ann Brown
(Bold Productions, 1987)

Hanukkah Crafts
by Judith Hoffman Corwin
(Watts, 1996)

Hanukkah Fun: Crafts and Games
by Andrea Weiss
(Boyds Mills, 1992)

Holiday Crafts Kids Can Make
by Better Homes & Gardens Staff
(Meredith Books, 1992)

Ideas for Special Occasions
(Marshall Cavendish, 1991)

Jewish Holiday Crafts for Little Hands
by Ruth Esrig Brinn
(Kar Ben, 1993)

Kwanzaa Crafts
by Judith Hoffman Corwin
(Watts, 1995)

One Hundred Twenty-One Holiday Crafts Kids Can Make
by Highlights for Children Staff
(Highlights, 1993)

Thanksgiving Crafts
by Judith Hoffman Corwin
(Watts, 1995)

Thanksgiving Fun: Great Things to Make and Do
by Ronne Randall
(Kingfisher, 1994)

Valentine Crafts
by Judith Hoffman Corwin
(Watts, 1994)

Glossary

Allah The Arabic word for God.

ancestor A past member of a family.

calypso A West Indian song. It usually comments on local events.

commemorate To celebrate in memory of someone or something.

czar The name of the former rulers of Russia.

enlightenment A sudden moment of understanding or seeing the truth about something.

fast To go without food.

fertility The ability to produce good crops for the harvest.

festivity A celebration.

fiesta A religious festival held in Spanish-speaking countries.

founder A person who starts up an organization or leads a group of believers.

garland A circle of flowers that is used for decoration.

guru A religious teacher or leader of the Hindu religion.

icon A picture that is made to be used in worship.

maypole A tall pole decorated with flowers and ribbons. It is the centerpiece of special dances in some countries during May.

nirvana In the Buddhist religion, a feeling of perfect peace and of being blessed.

orthodox Strict and traditional.

replica An exact copy of something.

resurrection The return back to life after dying.

retablo A portable altar that consists of a box-shaped frame with decorated panels.

ritual A religious or very serious set of actions.

temperate Describes areas of the world with a mild climate.

wheat sheaf A stack made of bunches of wheat that have been cut during the harvest.

winter solstice The day in each year when it is dark for the longest period of time.

Index